D1612154

MINIMALISM

or

How to Simplify Your Life

Tobias Jan Pedersen

Table of Contents

Introduction

Can having less stuff make you a more joyful person? This is the question many of us ask ourselves at least a few times throughout our lives. Have you felt overwhelmed with all of your countless belongings? Do you wish you could wipe all your clutter away with a gust of wind?

Then a minimalist lifestyle is for you. To live like a minimalist doesn't mean living in a chic multimillion-dollar loft with only a set amount of furniture surrounded by vast empty spaces. Being a minimalist does, however, add more space to our daily lives and personal belongings and changes the way we see stuff and the stuff we bring and allow to remain in our lives and spaces.

We will start by thinking like a minimalist, don't worry, it's not complicated. We will think of the rewards and benefits of having less clutter and more space in our daily lives. This is quite true when looking at things from the bathroom to the garage. Here is where the fun starts; we will tackle room by room, ensuring each item has a proper place and positively contributes to the household.

Our goal is a clear, calm space that relaxes and revitalizes us. We will look at how being a minimalist impacts mental health and its effects on our environment. We will also set a daily routine so that we don't fall back into our hoarding ways.

Part One: The Philosophy Of Minimalism

Take Inventory of Your Possessions

Have a quick glance around you. In your line of sight, can you see twenty to thirty items that take up valuable space? Generally, you can separate these items into three categories, emotional, useful, and beautiful. Let's start with the most straightforward category: useful stuff.

These items are generally practical and functional and help us get things done like a well-placed rug or foot rest. Some of these items are essential for survival; others make our lives a little bit easier. It's enticing to think that all our stuff is helpful, but you'll be surprised to learn that is not always the case.

For example, It's pretty fascinating how little we need to keep ourselves alive:

- A simple shelter
- Clothing for body heat
- Water
- Food
- Cooking utensils and a few containers

Note: Anything other than these critical elements are items that are not necessary to our survival.

However, other items are still beneficial; some of these include:

- Sofas
- Beds
- Sheets
- Combs
- Pens
- Laptops
- Books
- Staplers
- Hammers
- Screwdrivers- you get the idea.

Defining the usefulness of an item in minimalist home design

Anything that you use daily or has some usefulness can be added to a minimalist household. But there is a catch; for something to be useful, you must use it. Many of us have things that can be useful, but we just don't use them.

Duplicates, for example, how many of those plastic containers make it out of your cupboard or into your freezer or lunch bag? Other things decay because they are too much of a burden to clean. This is where items begin to lose their usefulness.

Emotional stuff

Next, we have our emotional stuff, things that we have that we remember people, places, or events by. Those things have all the right to stay, as long as you don't feel obligated to like grandma's china tea set or dad's pipe collection, or perhaps something you crafted three years ago that has no meaning to you now.

Beautiful stuff

Lastly, we have beautiful things. These are items like paintings, vases, ornaments, etc., things that give you some kind of joy having them around or looking at. If it's collecting dust or just sitting in the attic, consider it clutter.

You are More than Your Possessions

Sometimes we get influenced by advertisers. Here we'll have to create another category; aspirational stuff, things we buy to impress others. We may not accept it, but you probably got all those things to project a particular image. Take cars, for example; we can get an average car that can get us from point A to B.

Instead, we get a brand new luxury car that's double or even triple the price because we are trying to acquire a particular status image. It doesn't stop there, of course. Keeping up with all the trends that can just change a minute after purchase, buying name-brand clothes when regular clothes do the job just as well.

We don't need designer handbags or the best lipstick to be a model. Aspirational stuff is just another version of ourselves and us wanting others to take notice. We need to clean this clutter out, so we have the time, energy, and space to realize our true selves and full potential.

Less clutter is less strain

Think of all the energy you spent looking after one object in your home; now add all your belongings to the list; that is physically exhausting. Being a caretaker of all your things can be a full-time job. With the amount of time and money we spend on our stuff, we might think our property owns us instead of it being the other way around.

We've likely all seen something in the store, and we just couldn't see ourselves living without it. Next, you have the stress of not getting the item; you don't know anyone who will give us one, so you will have to buy your own thus, you will take it home.

Now you are obligated to clean it regularly because dirt and dust might shorten its lifespan.

You have to be relatively cautious when you use it so that it doesn't break or get ruined. Moreover, keep it out of reach from pets and children. After you purchase the item you have to take good care of it, after all, you spent good money on it. You did not just get a new object; you also got a lot of responsibility.

Having so many things to look after can take up quite a good amount of energy and time each day and can cause so much stress. Why have these items to look after when you can be spending your time with loved ones living a relatively stress-free life?

Sometimes fixing things that get broken can cost more than the actual item.

Let's imagine only having half your stuff. Wouldn't that be so much less strain and upkeep, meaning more time for ourselves and our loved ones, don't you think? That is the minimalist's way of life; you just need to put your stuff in the right place so that it does not control your life or get in your way.

Fewer Possessions = More Freedom

What if you suddenly get a job opportunity overseas and suddenly have to move in three days. Would you be excited to go, or would you look around your house and wonder how you will pack everything in time. How would you transport all your stuff across the vast ocean if you are even willing to do it by now?

You would probably decide it's not worth the effort, and maybe something else will come along. It's crazy to think our stuff has so much power over us. Things can tie us down and keep us from exploring new interests, and they can get in the way of family relationships and even your career.

Have you ever had to cancel a family visit because your house was too messy or full of clutter, or even say no to going on a vacation? Clutter can also weigh on our spirits. We can feel lazy and tired in a cluttered room, and we can't get things done. Without the burden of all our possessions weighing us down, we'll have energy and be ready for anything.

Out of sight, out of mind

Out of sight and mind doesn't work either; we need to get rid of all stuff that weighs us down mentally. There's abundantly more we could be doing than paying off credit card bills. Traveling is part of minimalist living; think about the pain of having so many suitcases when you only need a few items.

Imagine carrying a light backpack; you can stash it in a locker when you don't want to carry it to museums and tourist sites. Having less stuff can add so much more freedom to your daily life. Freedom to take your dog for a walk or even go to the park and relax in the sun.

Or even to read a book or do something you always wanted to do. Now you have all the time you need to go on a holiday instead of maintaining all your countless belongings that were just taking up all of your valuable time. You will additionally have more opportunities to experience life and all its wonders.

Become less sentimental

Developing a non-sentimental attitude will make it so much easier to declutter our home. Not to mention the pain when you lose your stuff or it gets taken from you, like in the event of thefts, fires, and floods. That's why you need mental exercise so that your stuff doesn't have a hold over you.

Visualize

Let's start with something easy. Imagine life without our stuff; you don't need to imagine it; you can actually remember it. Many of us remember our early adult lives, such carefree times. All of our possessions could fit in just a few bags. You didn't have to stress about going to the dry cleaners, doing car maintenance, or home repairs.

Many of us get to re-experience a space-free life when we go on vacation once or twice a year. Take camping, for example. You had everything you needed for survival and comfort. You didn't care how you looked, and the clothes you had on did their job. You cooked your supper on a pan over the open fire and ate with nothing more than a plate, cup, and fork.

Your tent was simple and kept you warm and dry. What you had was just enough for your needs leaving enough time for you to relax and enjoy nature. Using that as a reference, ask yourself what is worth keeping and what do you feel sentimental about? Chances are it's not the object but rather a person; however, if it's the object itself, it's worth keeping.

Save pictures digitally

Save your photos online. You don't need all those photo albums taking up all that space. You can do the same with paperwork unless you need the original copy.

Do you really need it

Pass on heirlooms if you don't feel you need them. You can always keep a scrapbook of all the clutter you want to revisit but don't want to keep around; a scrapbook can always be passed onto the next generation and helps revisit past memories.

Take a break from routine

Take a break from your normal routine, like a vacation. This way, you can weaken the power your stuff has over you and truly see it for what it is. Just more clutter.

Be the Warden of Your Possessions

Be your own warden and control how much of an object or item you have. You don't need twenty pairs of shoes or a closet full of clothes. Think of minimalism; control what you buy and the amount you buy. Limit yourself to how each item fits into your daily life and if you have the space for it.

Simply put, we get our things one of two ways it's given to us or buy them. As you go through your house, ask yourself how each item ended up in your life. Was it given to me, or did I buy it? We just need to exercise complete control over our lives to ensure we only purchase items that hold usefulness in our lives.

Ask yourself the following question when you purchase an item. What value will it add to my home? Does it deserve a spot in your premises? Will the item make your life simpler, or do you have something else that can do the same task already? Would you want to keep it forever? If not, will it be hard to get rid of?

Learn to say no

Learning to say no, may come in handy more often than you think and not just when decluttering your home but at your workplace too. For instance, if you're going to a professional conference or meeting, examine the pamphlets or books there. If they make their way back home, give them to your coworkers or recycle them.

Handling gifts

Gifts, on the other hand, require different planning. What do you do with gifts that you want to keep? You can't let them pile up in your closets or in the back of the drawer; you are trying to remove all your clutter, after all. Keep a donation box somewhere close but not in your way, and put all your stuff that you don't want or need in there.

Once it's full, you can give the box to a local charity. Taking a picture of the gift also works just as well. Just take the picture with your favorite sweater or scarf on, and do a little pose. Send the photo to those who gave you the gift and donate the sweater to charity. If you are lucky, everyone will be happy.

To be a good warden of your possessions, you have to think of your home as a sacred space, not a storage space. You don't have to provide housing for every item that you cross paths with. If an item has no value or beauty in your home, it's unnecessary. Refusing items early on will save you space later.

Embrace a clutter-free space

Too much clutter can often put our lives in discomfort, making us less creative. On the contrary, if we have more space, we can live more balanced. A cluttered room can usually lead to a cluttered mind. Let's say you're sitting on your couch one day reading a book, and your eyes suddenly find something broken in the corner of the room.

You start to wonder if you will have enough time to fix it before supper. Your mind will distract you and your thoughts. Space is nothing really, but we never seem to have enough of it, space in our drawers, closets, or even garages. All of the space that was there when we first moved into our houses is now full of clutter, all because we put value into our stuff and not our space.

You just have to get rid of a few items, and you will have some much-needed space again. You don't need to fill up your home with many things just because you live in a big house. If you want to dance, you need space; you can also do more home exercises.

Space can also be seen as space between your daily activities; you can relax and have fun more often with your family, go outdoors and see nature, or even go rock climbing now that you have so much newfound time.

Having Less is Actually More

Finding joy in owning less is key in our minimalist home. Instead of buying gym equipment and not leaving your home, go to the gym or to the spa, maybe even for a walk. You don't need to maintain all of that equipment; this way, you can enjoy those activities without making space to store them.

Apply the same thing to your backyard for even less fret and effort. You don't need to put up a flower show. Just keep it clean and maintained by letting the professional landscapers do the hard work for you. In this way, you won't have to own all the equipment and conduct all the upkeep when they are available. Go to your local pool if you want to relax.

You can apply window shopping to your life if you like to spend a lot. Think of it as an outing to the museum. You get to admire it, love it, and then move on. You can get the same feeling from looking at things rather than owning them.

On your adventure to becoming a minimalist or perhaps more of a minimalist, you want to reduce the number of things you own in your house and the amount of time and energy they require from you. You can do so by moving your interests and activities into the public world; you can become more socially active rather than sitting and caring for your stuff.

Living Content in Your Means

What's enough for you might just not be enough for the next guy. Most of us would agree that we have enough shelter, clothing, food, and enough water for our basic needs. So why do we still want to buy more? According to the dictionary, " enough means to satisfy a desire or need for the want. But here's the problem: our needs have been satisfied, but our desires and wants haven't.

Once we have what we need for survival, our happiness is just the amount of stuff we own. We just need to remain focused on what we own and not what we don't own. Go through your home and make a list of all your possessions. Can you still say you don't have enough?

Simplicity is Key for Minimalist Living

You must realize your actions have consequences for the world. If you know someone is dying of thirst, would you still be running the water when you brush your teeth in the mornings? If you got to experience deforestation firsthand, would you still go and build a large house? Perhaps you would live a bit more lightly if you saw how your life impacts other people and their lives.

Everything you buy uses some of the earth's resources. The less we need to survive, the easier it is on the planet for the next generations. You should use products with reusable containers or biodegradables and reduce your consumption. You know it's practically impossible to calculate the human and environmental impact of each and every item you buy.

However, you can always buy locally instead of having your fruits and vegetables imported, and if you buy locally, your hard-earned money stays in your communities. Moreover, you can go to a second-hand shop instead of going to the mall. Limit what you buy; if you don't need more shoes or shirts, don't buy more; it's pretty simple.

Part Two: Live Without Resistance

Step One: Start fresh

It's always tricky to know where to start any task. We see heaps of stuff in our closets, drawers, cupboards, and on our counters. We might also have things that are out of sight, for example, storage units, garages, or even basements. However, decluttering doesn't happen overnight.

It takes time to get rid of things, and as we progress with it, it becomes fun. The experience you get from decluttering feels like a weight lifted off your shoulders.

Now that we are starting fresh. We are going to do the same for each area of our homes. We are not getting rid of our possessions; we are just going to relocate them into another open space.

If you want to start over, take each drawer or closet and empty all its contents. For drawers, you can turn them upside down and unload all of the contents. If it's a closet, make sure there are only shelves left after you're done taking out all your stuff. Each room must be empty, and nothing can stay.

We will relocate all our possessions to the porch or another open space to allow for easier sorting. It's much easier to declutter if you decide what stays and not what you are getting rid of. What we have around us tells our story.

Step Two: Categorize your belongings

We are going to categorize our belongings into three groups. Trash, Treasure, and Transfer. You will need a large refuse bag for the first one and boxes for the other two, or whatever you find easier to use. You can keep an extra box in case you can't decide on some things.

As you search through your stuff, you'll find things you're unsure of and any items you might just want to keep. Put it in the box labeled unsure, and if you haven't gotten back to it within a year or so. Give these items to charity. It's about saving space from things you surely don't need.

First up is the trash pile; this is easy, everything from garbage to broken items that you can't fix again. Do remember to recycle if possible, and keep your environment in mind. You can always give someone else something if you think it can be used elsewhere.

Next is the treasure pile for all the things you want to keep and cherish. If you haven't used something in over a year, it probably doesn't belong here. We surely don't want to give away our valuable space to items that don't deserve it. You certainly don't want to keep things like collectibles and decorations if you're not displaying them with pride.

Lastly is the transfer pile. Here are all the things that are still perfectly good but just not for you. You don't have to feel guilty about letting your stuff go; give them a new life and purpose someplace else. Don't feel the need to keep something just because you might need it again; if it's not used, you don't need it.

Step Three: The sentiment behind each possession

As you go through your belongings, ask yourself, what is the reason for a particular item being part of your household. It must make a positive contribution in order to stay. Sometimes you might have doubles or something that looks similar to what you own.

Being a minimalist is about having enough and not extra. In some cases, you might have bought something, and you decide to keep the old one just in case; in other cases, it might have been through gifts.

Once you've gotten rid of all the duplicates, ask yourself how often you use each item and how much. If you use it regularly, it should be by your treasure pile, but if you can't answer these questions, then it can't be close to your treasure pile unless it's valuable to you and the space it occupies.

While you're busy decluttering, you'll find multiple reasons for keeping something. As you declutter, keep the 20/80 rule in mind. 20% of our stuff gets used 80% of the time. That means you can get by with a fifth of all your belongings and not even notice it.

Step Four: Maintaining order

Stray things can't wander into your house when each item needs a designated spot in your household. When assigning places to your possessions, keep in mind how often you use things. If it's on a regular basis, keep things close, so you don't have to search for it. If you don't use it often, it certainly shouldn't be in your way; store it where it's not in the way but still easily accessible.

Divide your house into zones, kitchen zone, bathroom zone, living room zone, and bedroom zone. Each of these zones can be further broken down; within the kitchen zone, you have the cleaning, eating, and preparation zones. Within the bathroom zone, you have bathing and grooming zones. Within the living room zones, you have the computer, hobby, and television zones.

If you stand in one of your zones and stretch your arms out, the area around you can be defined as your inner circle. Your easily accessible things, like dishwashing liquid, toothpaste, underwear, and checkbook, should be in your inner circle. Your outer circle should contain things like cleaning supplies and toiletries. This is usually your cupboards, lower or higher shelves, closets, and under your bed.

A pretty good thing to keep in mind is if something is used less than once a week, but more than once a year, it belongs in your outer circle. Lastly, we have deep storage. This is generally outside your living space, like the garage, attic, or basement. Here you store things like spare parts, seasonal decorations, and other things you use once a year. However, don't let deep storage accumulate all the unwanted stuff you don't ever use, donate or get rid of them if you don't use them.

Remember that decorative items can be displayed if they're truly special to you. You don't have to push it aside. The whole point of these items is so you can see them; if you store them in a box in the basement, you should probably question yourself and ask why you still have them. The more space we have, the more we feel the need to stuff it with priceless items, but having more space is actually an asset, not a liability.

Step Five: Living clutter-free

Flat surfaces are a magnet for clutter. When a seemingly vast uncluttered surface surrounds you, it can be so easy to place objects down and then forget about them. Having a clear surface is where the magic happens. Think of all the things we can do with a clear area.

We can prepare a glorious meal in a clean area, but we can't do much in a cluttered place. All we need is a new attitude, and we'll conquer our surface clutter. Open surfaces are not for keeping items. Keep all surfaces clean for activity, not storage.

Follow these principles, and your home will look organized and neater, and it will be so much easier to clean. If you choose to keep decorative items, keep them limited to three or four; you don't want all your space getting wasted by decorations that you don't feel the need to save. After we've spent all our time decluttering, we also have to make an effort to keep it clean. Surely you don't want to repeat all that hard work.

Step Six: Staying organized

Here we are going to learn how to achieve our minimalist goals by learning valuable tips on how to combat clutter and keep our stuff under control. The idea was to create zones throughout our homes and assign each item to that zone instead of it ending up all around our homes.

We will create "modules" to organize and sort our stuff. The module concept comes from systems design. It just means we divide complex systems into smaller, task-specific parts. In the same way, our households are just as tricky, with lots of things to store and keep track of. For this purpose, a module is a bunch of items that get a particular task done.

For example, decorating a cake or paying the bills. We will have to gather all the stuff with similar functions, store these items together so that they are easily accessible, and get rid of the rest that doesn't fit with it. The first step is to gather all the same items and store them together, like spices, photos, hardware, and crafting materials; you get the concept.

Gathering all of the same stuff in one place will let you see how much you have. When you've gathered all twenty-nine of your blue or black pens, you will notice you don't need to buy more. You will also know not to bring home more duplicates of things you already own in the future. Once you've gathered all objects of the same group together, you can get rid of all the extras.

As you go through all of your items, you will come across excess supplies of certain things; cut it down to what you use now and what you realistically can use in the future. Go through your collection and only save what you favor. Apply the same thing to your cups, containers, shirts, socks, all the things you have an abundant amount of.

Lastly, you just have to contain all your possessions, don't let them spread through your house again. We think that by putting all our stuff in containers, it'll look neat and serene, but if we don't sort the rest from the trash, we'll just be going around in circles. Instead, declutter as much as you can before putting anything into a box or container. By creating our modules, we eliminate excess and make our possessions equivalent to our needs.

Step Seven: Limiting your possessions

By creating limits, we keep our possessions in check. Limits help you get the upper hand over your things; this way, you'll have more space, more control, and more power over each item. Let's take books as an example. We all know how fast they can accumulate.

We buy one, we read it, and now it has a permanent spot in our home. Storing all these books doesn't make you smarter; it just adds more clutter. Instead of keeping each book you've ever read, apply a limit. Keep the ones you enjoyed, and as you acquire more books, cull some of the other ones you haven't opened in a while.

Give them to a friend or family, or you can even donate them to your local library.

Limits can be applied to just about everything. Limit the number of shoes, socks, pots, chairs, candles, and collectibles you own. Not only does setting limits help you, but it can also help other family members get into the minimalist lifestyle.

Explain to your family members that each item has allocated space, and if things overflow, they must be cut down. The size of your house is the ultimate limit for our stuff. Stuff expands to fill space that's available. We think limits will suffocate, but it's actually liberating if you apply limits to your daily life.

Limiting our activities will free up more time for ourselves and our families. Limiting how much we spend can boost your bank balance, and it can cut credit card bills. Limiting yourself to eating healthy foods instead of fatty and sugary foods can improve your health. The possibilities are endless.

Step Eight: The one in one out rule

Sometimes we declutter, and nothing seems to happen. We can't understand how this is happening when we've filled up bags of stuff we don't need anymore.

Think of your house as a bucket of water. Decluttering is like making a hole in the bottom of the bucket, causing the bucket to empty drip by drip as you get rid of unwanted things.

Your stuff level should steadily decrease as long as you keep up the excellent work.

Here's the catch, if you don't stop pouring more stuff into the top, the stuff level will never go down. Every item that enters your house flows into the bucket. If you still continue shopping and acquiring things, the bucket will never decrease; in fact, it might just overflow.

This problem can be solved by following the one-in-one-out rule. Every item that enters your home, something similar must also leave. This will ensure your household doesn't flood and slow the progress you are making. For each new shirt you buy, you must get rid of an old one. Be reasonable; you can't get rid of socks because you got a fresh coat, or trading a paperclip for an office chair won't work either.

The one in one out strategy helps you get rid of all the rejects. As soon as something new enters your home, you can say farewell to the old one. Commit yourself to get rid of items first and then getting the new one; otherwise, you might not get rid of the old one.

Stick to the program so your household can enter a steady state where you don't own more than you currently need. As you continue to decrease your stuff, you will see a decrease in your stuff level. The more things you get rid of, the more rewarding the results are gonna be.

Step Nine: Reduce your available options

In the previous chapter, we learned that If you buy a new item, you get rid of the old one. With this system in place, we can get closer to our minimalist goals as we get rid of our items. We will have to give up our decluttering efforts to get even more done. Owning just enough and nothing more.

We have one mission when it comes to stuff in our drawers and closets, narrow it down. In a way, we want to reduce our property to the bare necessities. Keep in mind the basic necessities can mean different things to different people. Our personal needs depend on various things, like age, gender, peers, families, occupation, climates, and hobbies.

There is no master's list of what is in a minimalist household; you have to make your own list of must-haves and then narrow your stuff to match that list. When you choose an item, stop and ask yourself do you need it and can you get by without it? When you discover you have multiples of the same thing, get rid of the excess ones immediately.

There is good news, though; as we progress on our minimalist journey, we will discover our "necessities" will slowly become less. You can always use items with multi-function over single-function ones, for example, a sleeper couch instead of an extra guest bed.

Our objective is to get multiple things done at the same time with the least amount of items. And don't forget to favor versatile ones over specialty ones. Things with memories behind them can be challenging to part with as we are happily narrowing down our items. Instead of saving the whole thing, keep a piece. If an item's purpose is to recreate memories, you can use a smaller portion of it.

As you are decluttering, you can always take photos of items, then get rid of the things and use the images to preserve memories, and it doesn't take up space. Embrace minimalist living wholeheartedly, and you'll find yourself searching for ways to narrow your stuff down. It may come as quite a shock to you what we can do without certain things.

Step Ten: Declutter your digital life

Just like everyday clutter, digital clutter can make your life complicated or even stressful. Unorganized emails, duplicate files, and games can add up over time, filling our storage. Get into the habit of decluttering your device once or twice a month; this way, you'll have more space.

Get rid of all the unused apps or software. Your device will run smoother and faster, and you will be surprised at how much space gets used by apps you don't even realize you have anymore. Organize all your apps into separate folders, each folder with its own use.

Check your emails and at least declutter your inbox once a day. Having too many emails can cause confusion, and you might just forget an essential email with all the other ones distracting you.

Limit your screen time and how much you go on to social media per day. We want our freedom back from our devices. Keep it out of sight when you're at work so that you don't feel tempted to check it the whole time.

Tips to keep your digital life organized

Here are some tips:

- Get rid of contacts you no longer use or recognize.
- Limit your screen time and make sure you take a 5-minute break every hour; your eyes will thank you in the future.
- Set a time in your daily schedule when you want to check your emails at a particular time to take away the temptation to check your phone all the time.
- Limit yourself to one screen per day.
- Go for a walk in fresh air once a day or twice a day to ensure you don't stare at a screen for too long.

Step Eleven: The importance of daily upkeep

Once you've imported all of the steps from

- Start fresh,
- Categorizing your belongings
- The sentiment behind each possession

- Maintain order
- Live clutter-free
- Stay organized
- Limit your possessions
- The one-in-one-out rule
- Reduce your available options
- Declutter your digital life

- we simply can't just return to our old ways and call it a day.

We need to keep up and do everyday maintenance. We can't just have one declutter session and then end it there. If so, we might just suffer a rebound effect and accumulate more clutter. You must approach minimalist living the same way as a new healthy diet, not as some once-off activity.

We must stay vigilant about what enters our homes. We can't let things get out of control to maintain our minimalist lifestyle. Establish a routine to handle incoming stuff, like gifts, mail, and freebies, and stick to it. Place donation boxes by the front door; for example, it works wonders and prevents clutter from piling in other places.

Once something stays for a while, clutter soon follows. Think about it: there's a difference between a surface with nothing on it and one with something on it.

Sometimes we have to deal with other people's clutter; just return it to its rightful owner if you can't get rid of it.

Finally, don't stop decluttering. As you keep on decluttering, you might find things that survived the first round but don't seem to have a place in the second or third—Declutter in stages. Have a look in a few weeks or months again. You will see your things with new eyes.

Instead of getting rid of a lot of items per day, use the one-a-day rule, get rid of one thing per day. It can be anything from a book you will never read again to a pair of worn-out socks. It takes little effort or time, and at the end of each year, our homes will have 365 items less.

Part Three: From One Room To The Next

This next section focuses on the kitchen and dining room, bedroom, wardrobe, storage areas, bathroom, living, and family room (or what you may call your sitting room), office and your gifts, sentimental objects, and heirlooms.

But before we begin first, we will take a look at cleaning the spaces (this is a necessary step before you start to declutter) and what goes into minimizing your area based on the nine principles of interior design before we look at how to go about organizing each room.

Nine Steps to Speed Clean Your Home

Before you begin the decluttering process you will want to have a clean area to work in. As such before you begin you should take a few moments to speed clean the areas of your home you will be decluttering. Below you will discover nine simple steps to speed clean your home.

Step One: Gather all your necessary supplies

When cleaning anything, you will first need to gather all the necessary cleaning supplies to execute the job. You can easily cut down on your cleaning time by having all your cleaning tools and liquids in one place(like a basket or caddy). For instance, your cleaning supplies should include the basics like a microfibre cloth, sponge, paper towels, all-purpose cleaner, and a vacuum or broom.

Step Two: Remove all clutter

In the next step, you will need to go around the room with a basket and grab all the items that don't belong in that particular room. For instance, this can include things like toys, shoes, and mugs or glasses when cleaning the living room. Don't worry about that basket; you will get to it later.

Step Three: Fold or remove blankets

If your family members are prone to the cold, you may constantly have to remove or fold blankets and relocate them to the appropriate area. If any blankets are lying about, fold them and place them in their designated spot.

Step Four: Straighten any furniture

Start in the corner of your home and make your way through your house, straightening any out-of-place furniture and fluffing any cushions as you go along. You can additionally use a rag or small cloth to wipe away any surface spots. If you have time left over, you can vacuum the cushions too.

Step Five: Dust surfaces

When dusting, it is essential to use a microfiber cloth or an electrostatic duster. This is to ensure that all loose dust is swiftly collected.

Step Six: Grab the broom or vacuum

Once all your furniture is in its correct place, you can now proceed to give your home a quick sweep or vacuum.

Step Seven: Wipe away any visible dirt

Now that you have dusted the area and swept away any surface dirt, the next thing to tackle is the dirty floors that have collected dirt, crumbs, grime, and dust. It is vital to give them a once over now and again. You can do this with warm, sudsy water and a sponge or cloth to maintain their clean appearance. Ensure that you go over any clearly visible or sticky marks or spots.

Step Eight: Clean any glass or metallic surfaces

When it comes to cleaning up, most of us overlook our glass or metallic surfaces. So, grab that glass or surface cleaner and spray it into a microfibre cloth or rag. You will use a minimal amount of product by spraying the cleaner on a rag or microfibre cloth beforehand. What's more, you will be able to focus the product on the area that needs it the most.

Step Nine: Finish up

Now that you have quickly cleaned the space, you can begin to start the decluttering process. You can start this by focusing on that first basket of items you collected from step one before moving on with the rest of the decluttering.

The Nine Principles Of Interior Design

When looking at how to minimalize your space, one should first get familiar with the nine principles of interior design. By becoming familiar with these principles, you will have the prerequisite knowledge to accurately and effectively redesign your interior space (should you be willing to undergo the redesign process) to achieve a minimalist lifestyle.

Principle One: Invest in quality fixtures

Using quality fixtures like high-grade storage units, designer light fittings, and contemporary gas fires is an impressive way to decorate without adding clutter.

Principle Two: Choosing assorted materials

You can offer texture by using various materials in a traditional minimalist design, such as glass, timber cloth canvas, and pottery. This design style is all about joining function and form.

Principle Three: Select a piece of furniture to stand out

If you're stuck and don't really know where to start, choose a piece of furniture and build a story around it with plants, pottery, and art.

Principle Four: Let a piece of artwork dominate.

Get a supersized artwork and use it as the main vision point to create an eye-catching design. This will incorporate color and life into the overall look of your space.

Principle Five: Accent elements can be added

Mix up your neutral decor with elements of contrasting color, Like a piece of furniture, artwork, or a feature wall. Adding accent elements is kind of like giving a room a surprise. It's an easy way to draw attention to something instead of it getting lost in the crowd.

Principle Six: Keep your furniture simple

With the amount of furniture available today, it's easy to get carried away when choosing furniture. With the minimalist approach, it's sensible to downplay the furniture, choose something simple in design, and let other elements take the stage like a piece of art.

Principle Seven: Let the view speak for itself

If your home has a beautiful view, you can make that your center of attention. Keep your furniture simple and remove items you don't use. Use one or two indoor plants and some design-fitting artwork.

Principle Eight: Allow open space

Avoid trying to fill all the space with furniture just because there is plenty to fill. The idea is to keep your area open regarding minimalist design. Keep in mind that when it comes to minimalism, space is valuable.

Principle Nine: Use light as a means of decoration

Think outside the box and use beautiful lighting. On the other hand, chandeliers may be a minimalist's worst nightmare, but there are stunning lights out there that you can use to achieve a minimalist aesthetic. Use hanging drop lights as an example or even frosted pendant lights to add a Scandi look.

Room by Room

Kitchen and dining room

The kitchen is the most frequented room (apart from the bathroom) in our homes, and it can be one of the most frustrating spaces to keep organized. By using the less is more philosophy and following the steps in part two, you can create a beautiful, clutter-free kitchen where your whole family can enjoy spending their time. Moreover, below we will also look at seven tips to create a minimalist kitchen.

Seven tips for creating a minimalist kitchen:

Tip One: Get rid of all the clutter

The First step is to get rid of all clutter. And this doesn't mean you have to get rid of only the old magazine, newspapers, or bills piling on the counter. Instead, look at things like fruit baskets, small appliances, and other decorative items that reside in the kitchen, and see what you can put away. The key to minimalist decor is to create as much empty space as possible.

Tip Two: Change your color scheme

If you are ready to design a minimalist kitchen, rethink your color scheme. Use a neutral color palette for this decorating theme. Using neutral colors not only makes the room look simpler but also more spacious than it actually is.

Tip Three: Choose quality over quantity

Quality over quantity is the most critical minimalist living tip, and it goes hand in hand with your kitchen design. Invest in one or two quality items that will last you decades instead of buying the cheap and trendy kitchen utensils, appliances, or furniture that will quickly deteriorate and take up space once they are no longer in use.

Tip Four: Maximize storage space

Having a minimalist design does not imply that you have to get rid of your necessities and belongings to achieve the look. A minimalist kitchen uses smart storage units that homeowners can use to store their everyday appliances, coffee makers, and spices. Use this storage to free up precious counter space.

Tip Five: Use multi-function furniture

Using decor and function is crucial in a minimalist interior design. When choosing furniture, choose something that is versatile and can serve various functions.

Making use of a large kitchen island is one of the best features. It serves both as a dining area and food prepping zone; aside from having multiple functions, the kitchen island can also serve as the kitchen's focal point.

Tip Six: Keep your design simple

Minimalism is about simplicity and should be reflected in all aspects of your kitchen design, including furniture, storage, and decor. For instance, when choosing built-in cabinets, go for solid-colored doors with no handle or knobs. If you don't want plain cabinets, you can use a simple bar instead of the traditional knob.

Tip Seven: Choose statement-making furniture

Make sure that everything you incorporate has a design impact on the room and is functional for the space. Each piece of furniture, from the dining chairs to the hanging lights, must add a sense of style and personality to the space and be useful.

Bedroom

So you're ready to begin designing the minimalist bedroom of your dreams, but you don't really know where to start. Or you're concerned that you will have to spend a small fortune just to achieve the minimalist bedroom feel. Transforming your bedroom into a minimalist bedroom doesn't have to be time-consuming or expensive. Through some careful planning and organizing, as well as following the steps laid out in part two, you can create a minimalist bedroom in no time without spending buckets full of cash.

Here are ten tips for creating a minimalist bedroom.

Tip One: Get rid of all your junk

It's time for your junk to go, seriously, though. Carefully hunt through your bedroom belongings and put away anything you don't find meaningful. This goes for random wall hangings, collectible items or photos, and anything else. Remember that you are making space for things that truly matter to you when you sort through your bedroom debris.

Tip Two: A cold, threadbare space isn't what minimalism is about

Minimalism is about decluttering. Decluttering your wardrobe and really just getting rid of any unwanted stuff. It's about simplifying our surroundings and our lives. You shouldn't sacrifice all your warmth and coziness by getting rid of everything while creating a perfect minimalist bedroom.

Remember where you are in the middle of the decluttering process. Your bedroom should look and feel like a place where you want to spend most of your time because you do.

Tip Three: Choose a simple bed frame or go frameless

It will make quite the difference in the world by picking the right bed frame for the particular minimalist feel you are going for. A perfect minimalist bed frame will really set the tone for the whole room's atmosphere since your bed is typically the primary focal point of your bedroom. A platform bed, box spring, or metal bed frame are all excellent choices for a minimalist bed.

Tip Four: Use neutral-colored bedding

To achieve an authentic minimalist feel in your bedroom, use neutralized tones, like pale grays, creamy whites, or soft beiges. Remember, it's all about returning to the basics; too many clashing colored patterns won't give you the relaxing vibe you're after. Plus, by using a neutral color palette, you'll be able to add splashes of accent color at a later stage.

Tip Five: Purchase everything neutral

When you buy a new piece for your bedroom, make sure it fits with the neutral color palette. Once again, the aesthetic you're working so hard to create will be ruined by color clashes, so try to keep it within the color scheme you already decided upon.

Tip Six: Add more natural light

Incorporating lighting in a minimalist bedroom is almost an accessory on its own. Lighting can make a big difference in a room with the least amount of furniture available. Clear away curtains to bring in a large amount of natural light into your bedroom, if you can. This will assist you in making the room feel more minimal and open, adding a modern feel to it.

Tip Seven: Hang a piece of art you love

The idea to fill each wall with paintings or photos for the room to feel complete isn't part of the minimalist idea or aesthetic. Instead, use a single piece of art you will enjoy seeing whenever you enter your bedroom. Don't overfill the walls with paintings or photos because just as the bed acts as the focal point in the bedroom, so does whatever hangs above it.

Tip Eight: Add a bit of green in the form of plants

An excellent way to add a bit of color to a neutralized room is by adding a well-placed plant. Just make sure the plant doesn't crowd your artwork or vice-versa. Try a rubber plant for a modern-looking feel, as these artificial plants require little to no maintenance. A bouquet of freshly picked flowers will also work nicely; just ensure they're in a clear or neutral-toned vase.

Tip Nine: Try only using a single dresser or chest of drawers

Using only a single dresser or a set of drawers will make your bedroom look neat and uncluttered. If you can't seem to get this done, try keeping your dressers as far away from your bed as possible. You want the space around your bed to be free and simplistic.

Tip Ten: Use one shelf for chosen photos or books

If you are one such individual who likes to keep sentimental items in plain sight, you don't have to get rid of them on your minimalist journey; just limit yourself to one shelf so they don't take up unnecessary space.

Wardrobe

It's time to take on the clutter in our closets. This section is for you if you have many clothes and don't know what to wear. We will explore ways to cut down our wardrobe following the steps mentioned in part two and still have something to help us look well dressed. All the while saving money, time, and space. Here are seven tips for creating your very own minimalist wardrobe.

Tip One: Take out everything from your closet and dressers

Coats, shoes, rain jackets, pajamas, slippers, socks, take out everything, whether it's on a hook, shelved, or stuffed in the very back of your closet, it must all come out; only shelves and hanger railings should be left. Place all your clothes on your bed. If your bed doesn't fit all of your clothes, do it in stages instead.

After you've taken out all your clothes, start sorting them into things you wear regularly and things you think need a better home or you don't have a use for it anymore. We will get to the sorted clothes at a later stage.

Tip Two: Discover your own style

It's crucial that we feel comfortable and confident in our clothes. When creating your minimalist wardrobe, ditch all the trendy seasonal clothes and create your own style that is unique to you. An authentic, timeless wardrobe will make you feel most like yourself and reflect your personality.

Ask yourself: Which fabrics do I feel most comfortable wearing? Which accessories, colors, and patterns best compliment my personality and reveal my true self? What do my clothes say about me? Ask yourself these simple yet necessary questions to ensure that your wardrobe and clothing suit your style and needs.

Tip Three: Try shopping secondhand

No surprise here; the biggest hindrance to building a minimalist wardrobe is the cost. Quality clothes cost more because they're made of better, longer-lasting fabric. Still, some of these expensive pieces can be way out of our reach, so here are a few beginner tips :

Shop secondhand

Thrift stores are famous for selling cheap clothing and worn-out furniture. We discovered some of our most timeless and favorite pieces on the racks of some of these thrift stores, and they can be cheaper at times.

Save for big-ticket items

You don't have to go out and replace your entire wardrobe all at once. Start small and save months in advance for those expensive items, such as winter coats, high-end denim, or fine minimalist jewelry. When creating your minimalist wardrobe, remember one thing, you're paying for quality rather than quantity. It can seem less daunting when looking at the bigger picture and how much money you will save over time.

Shop for deals

There are copious environmentally conscious brands that provide coupon codes and discounts when you sign up for their newsletters.

Tip Four: Stop being overly sentimental

You know what I'm talking about. That one dress brings back so many happy memories; you still have to get rid of it, though. Get rid of the clothes but keep the pictures, for example, wedding dresses and prom clothes. You're probably not going to wear those items again. It's time to get it out of your home. Donate your wedding dress and unwanted clothing to a worthy cause.

Tip Five: Has it been worn recently

Go through your sweaters first, then move on to items like pants, undergarments, shoes, etc.; get rid of the ones you haven't worn this season; even the items your aunt bought for you that make you feel connected to her. Call her instead; this way, you save closet space, and connecting with family is a win-win.

Tip Six: Put everything back

See how much more space you have now that you have decluttered your closet. Now that you have removed all those unnecessary or unworn items from your area, do you not feel more organized and uncluttered?

Tip seven: Repeat the process as often as you need

Stuff can accumulate when you're paying attention and even more when you are not. Starting your minimalist wardrobe with a simple elimination method will help you keep the things you want and eliminate the rest; it sounds easier than it is. Make sure that you repeat the process every three months; otherwise, you're decluttering for no reason.

Storage areas

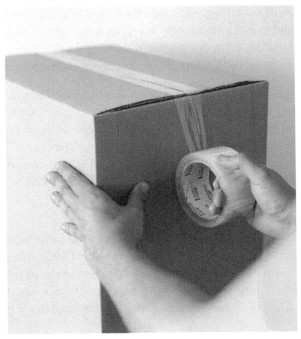

Now that we've taken care of our living spaces, let's take a look at our storage spaces. For example, our attics, garages, and basements are often where most of the clutter from the rest of the house ends up when we don't know what to do with it. But just because it's out of sight doesn't mean it's out of mind. By following these few tips and the aforementioned steps laid out in part two, you will regain your space and conquer the clutter.

Tip One: Start fresh

Imagine how orderly our lives would be if we had a huge basement or a two-car garage to put all our belongings in. But unfortunately, it doesn't work that way. Just because we have so much space doesn't mean we have to fill every corner of it with stuff. It's better to store your car or turn the place into a bedroom or family room.

Don't let your junk take up more space than intended. When starting fresh, you can either take one weekend and do the whole place or declutter a bit at a time. If you have a storage space outside your living place, get rid of it. It's like owning another house but just for your stuff.

Tip Two: Separate your stuff

Divide your stuff into three piles, one for things you want to keep, one for plain trash, and one for donations. Keep to a straightforward rule: out it goes if you don't use something more than once a year. These can be your holiday decorations like Christmas ornaments or Easter baskets.

Seasonal things like pool toys and sports equipment that are only used at certain times of the year can be added to the things you want to keep. Trash can vary from broken items that you've replaced by now but just forgot about them. For example, the old broken tv or chair that is just standing there gathering dust can be thrown away. And lastly, your donations are the items you don't have a use for anymore and can probably live without.

Tip Three: Why keep a particular item?

To keep the clutter entirely out, you must apply the same principles to our attics, basements, and garages as you do to your living space: save them for the things you use now, not the stuff you used in the past or might just use in the future. Use these types of spaces for things that help you get things done, like your lawnmower, gutter cleaner, and drain cleaner.

Things like your Christmas tree and Halloween decorations can stay since they serve a purpose. Question any heirlooms and gifts that have no place in your home if they have a place at all.

Tip Four: everything in its designated place

It's crucial that everything has a designated spot and is always returned to that spot. In this case, you don't have to search for something when you know exactly where it is. Plan the space out perfectly and create zones where you can store your items. For instance, create a gardening zone for all your gardening tools and appliances.

Create a holiday zone for all your Christmas, Easter, and Halloween decorations. Creating zones for all your items keeps them in one place and keeps clutter away from your storage places if used correctly.

Tip Five: Keep all surfaces clear

Keep anything that serves as functional space clear in your basement, attic, or garage, such as work benches or tables, free from clutter. The task performed in these areas can sometimes be dangerous; therefore, keeping the surface clean is an essential safety precaution. In other words, you don't want random objects getting in your way while working with a power saw or using other hazardous chemicals. Keep the floors clean as well; it can be tricky finding your way in the dark areas without light, and you can't trip over things that are out of place while carrying something heavy or moving something big.

Tip Six: Limit what you own

Limit your belongings to only the space that is provided in the garage attics or basements. By using only the shelves provided and taking the floor out of the equation, you'll remove a lot of potential clutter and free up space for other likely hobbies or activities.

You can always limit your possessions by categorizing them. For example, limit yourself to only one or two boxes of holiday decorations and only select your favorite pieces. And finally, limit yourself to only one or two boxes of sentimental stuff, like your old high school and college stuff, weddings, and so on. Apply the same limits to any heirlooms, souvenirs, baby keepsakes, children's art, trophies, and schoolwork you decide to store.

Tip Seven: The one in one out rule

Whenever you buy something new, always use the one-in-one-out rule. This means whenever you get something new, get rid of the old one that serves the same function. When you acquire a shiny new lawnmower or hedge trimmer, donate or sell the old ones; don't keep them.

Keeping items that no longer serve their function will mean they are just taking up unnecessary space, and it's undoubtedly just gathering dust. If it helps, pretending that you only have room for the one and can't keep the second one will help you overcome those hard choices.

And lastly all the furniture. Why keep furniture there if your basement, attic, or garage is not a living space? Unless you have plans for the piece of furniture, like giving it to a friend or family member, don't let it take up space and never be used again. Give it a new home at a charity instead of catering to its needs.

Bathroom

Ready for something relatively easy. Let's take the minimalist strategies that we've learned so far and beautify our bathrooms. This room is generally the smallest in our homes, with the least amount of storage space compared to the kitchen and living room. Decluttering it will be a breeze.

With a few simple habits and a little effort, we can create a space that soothes our souls while brushing our teeth. Follow these simple tips as well as the steps laid out in part two to make your very own minimalist bathroom.

Tip One: Start from scratch

Like in the other rooms, start by clearing out the contents of all the cabinets, shelves, or drawers. Clear everything off the countertops, and don't forget about the shower stall or tub. Take the shaving cream, soap, caddies, and razors out.

Carry it out of the bathroom and lay it on the dining room table or your bedroom floor. Decluttering is more effective when you remove items from their usual spot. As you go through each item, you'll determine what you need before putting only the useful things back.

Tip Two: Plan your design

Go for a concept, not a theme, if you want your bathroom to look like something out of a magazine. Add your own style to it; minimalism doesn't mean all white with a single piece of furniture in the room. Concrete is an excellent way to incorporate texture into a space and add a modern look. While incorporating a specific style, color, and texture, there are many ways to create a minimalist design.

Tip Three: Create a blank slate

Let's transform the space. Your walls should be simple; it doesn't have to be white. You can simply paint your walls white but if you like color, add some light color to make the space appear larger. If you're looking to add texture, consider tiles; either go for color, pattern, or shape; never all three.

You want the walls to almost disappear in a minimalist design. If you are thinking about adding a touch of color, then add a solid color tile without any drastic designs or shapes. Especially if you're choosing to go with a hexagon shape or a herringbone pattern.

Tip Four: Upgrade your existing features

This usually means making your tub, shower, and sink counter fit with your minimalist goals. Tubs are already minimalistic since they mostly come in white. But if you want to replace your current tub, go for a free-standing one or keep the shape simple. Since tiles have already been discussed, you can take your design further by adding a simple acrylic or glass shower door.

If a new shower door isn't an option, you can always go for a white shower curtain which can go a long way. When choosing what type of vanity design, it is best to opt for a straightforward and useful option. By going for square shapes, you create crisp and clean lines. You can get creative with the material and design here. Opting for a vanity means you will also have excellent storage properties. Keep that in mind when planning your layout.

Tip Five: Replace existing fixtures

Elegant plumbing fixtures are all the rage when incorporating minimalism. These include the faucet on your shower head and sink. You can achieve that well-designed, expensive look through streamlined fixtures. Here you can have some fun by playing with shape, gloss, and color to create a unique design that matches you. To achieve a well-rounded finish, it is vital to ensure that all your fixtures work well together.

Tip Six: Choose your decorations

Decorating a space is the fun part of redesigning a room. And to make a minimalist room feel like a home, you still need décor. Therefore, when it comes to minimalist decorating, the best thing is not to go to extreme lengths but instead to keep it simple.

Keep in mind your bathroom space; if you've added color to the walls, keep your decorations to that color scheme. When looking at minimalist design in the bathroom, if you have chosen to use a singular fixture as your centerpiece, it is essential to maintain a neutral color scheme.

Tip Seven: Be picky about what you add back into the space

With your minimalist bathroom done, it's time to add all your stuff back. This means towels, products, and toiletries. You can't slip up on this part; if your towels don't match your bathroom scheme get new ones; remember, white always fits. You took in mind storage, so toiletries and products should have their own place and won't pile on the shelves anymore.

Living and family room

It doesn't matter how your four walls are arranged—to best suit your purposes; it's the area where your family members gather and guests hang out when they visit you. In most dwellings, it's the most significant space and the one that sees the most action. Here you can use the steps laid out in part two and utilize the eight tips and ten steps found below to transform your living space.

Eight tips for creating a minimalist living room

Tip One: Start by decluttering

Once you begin pursuing a minimalist living room, you will first need to start by decluttering the area. While you do this, you should remember less is always more. The entire purpose of creating a simple living room is to have less. So, now is the time to eliminate any small things and other decorations that have made their home in your living room.

If you plan to keep most of these items around, your living room is bound to get cluttered. Therefore try and keep only the quintessential objects and articles in the space. If you pick it up and you no longer have a use for it, or you can live without it, then it's more than likely time for that item to go.

Tip Two: Consider the total size of the space

Factoring in the size of your space is a critical consideration when it comes to minimizing your living room. For example, you wouldn't want to place random pieces of furniture in your living room. Why? Well, simply speaking, it's only going to make the space feel more cramped.

Using different shapes and sizes of furniture, like an L shape couch, will not subtract from the amount of space available but rather leave enough space for other pieces of furniture. Just remember that the total size of the space matters; by switching things up, you can help make the area feel more open.

Tip Three: Add more green to your space

You might wonder how adding more green into your space will help declutter it. Truth be told, there really is nothing quite like adding some live plants to help make the room appear brighter, fresher, and cleaner. You can easily add to the brightness of your living room by adding two or three plants with bright green foliage around your living room.

You can even spruce it up by adding the plants in neutral planters or a beautiful glass vase depending on the size of the plant you have decided on. Additionally, you will need to ensure that the plants you have chosen have adequate light and shade, depending on their needs. If you need any assistance when selecting the right plant for your space, reach out to your local plant nursery.

Tip Four: Add floating shelves

Transforming your living room is as simple as adding some floating shelves. A simple floating shelf can make your living room feel both more modern and more organized. These handy shelving units can be used to store a small plant or two books and some well-placed ornaments. With the addition of floating shelves to your space, your living room should by default feel more contemporary, brighter, cleaner, and more organized.

Tip Five: Factor in your color choices

The idea of having an all-white color scheme featuring bare white walls, a white carpet/rug, and a white or cream-colored couch or armchair is appealing to all of us who are searching for a more airy and bright atmosphere. However, suppose an all-white aesthetic is not something you would be interested in, perhaps because of small children or animals.

In that regard, you can always opt for a few pieces of white furniture accompanied by more neutral-colored design elements. Incorporating a few bold colors either in the form of a bright woven rug, wall accents, or a vivid artwork into the neutral space is another option for creating a stylishly minimalist design.

What's more, you can also add differently textured or toned items into the mix by using varying hues of the same color for various things like your walls, carpet/rug, or other furniture. You can also brighten up your living space by sprucing up any bookshelf with a bit of color. With that said, organizing your books by color rather than by the author is an excellent way to add some flair or a pop of color to your living room.

Whichever option you decide to make use of, always ensure that it will flow well with the overall color palette. You wouldn't want to have a space that looks like it was haphazardly thrown together with multiple colors and textures, making your space feel tacky. As a pro tip, be sure to coordinate colors as much as possible.

Tip Six: Out of sight

Are you overwhelmed by a massive stack of bills, magazines, or an assortment of other random objects in your living room? Don't worry; you're probably not alone in this, as many of us are guilty of letting our possessions get the better of us. However, it's not too late to find a new home for such infrequently used items.

First, you will need to devise a sound plan to store items you will use again out of sight and items that are gathering dust, like those stacks of unused magazines that will need to be donated or recycled. Remember, you can use many storage vessels like a box, crate, or even a pretty basket/storage bin when storing items. Storing items that still have a use but aren't always useful is essential to ensuring your living room remains clutter-free.

Tip Seven: Everything in the space should function well

Set aside decluttering your space for now. Instead, focus on creating a space where all your belongings pair well with each other. This includes the color scheme, as these elements are crucial for going and attaining minimalism.

Although this will look different to everyone, typically speaking, your stuff should flow well together. For example, each piece- from your smallest vase to your largest couch should be classic, fit well with the color palette and be simple yet effective for maximum impact.

Tip Eight: Make use of the less is more mantra

Once you begin your transition into minimalist living, it can get overwhelming, especially when it comes time to officially part ways with some of your stuff. But remember living minimally doesn't mean you have to part ways with all your belongings. Specifically speaking, you can always do a test by storing some furniture or items temporarily to see if minimalism is the right approach for you.

Top tip- Minimalism is about simplicity; you can always get your stuff back, but having the less is more mindset will ensure you stay on the path of minimalist living.

10 Steps to help you design a minimalist living room

Step One: Eliminate any unnecessary furniture

One of the most critical mistakes you can make as a homeowner happens when you need to furnish your living room. Having too many furniture items can subtract from your living space's overall aesthetic. You may think that just because the space is there, you will need to fill it up, but you would be mistaken.

One of the critical minimalist design principles is to have enough space open to create a visual balance. This is key because, without it, you could end up with a room that feels closed off, confined, smaller than it actually is, and cluttered. Therefore to achieve a successfully furnished living room, focus on the critical principle listed below:

Use furniture that serves a purpose

Should you have ample space to work with, you just may feel tempted to fill it with all sorts of items. But when it comes to the design of your living room, it is best not to stray away from its intended function- a space that promotes relaxation, conversation, and social interaction.

However, if you have a living room on the larger side, you can split the space to serve two functions. For example, you could section off a portion of the living room to create a home office or perhaps add your dining table to create a space that functions as both the living room and dining room.

However, should you decide to add more furniture to support the secondary function of your living room, you will need to ensure that there is still ample space to move around and ensure that the furniture you add serves a purpose. Explicitly speaking, should you decide to incorporate additional chairs or benches, you can add them as a means of decorating instead of using them.

Moreover, haphazardly adding in random furniture items will end up causing a loss of function in your space. It's important to realize that a living room that functions as your office and a dining area is bound to be cluttered, feel cramped, and be visually confusing, thus taking away from its intended use.

Step Two: Pick a straightforward color scheme

Choosing the correct color is crucial for creating a comfortable and calm environment as well as promoting social interaction. Using a bold color scheme can subtract from the living room aesthetic as a whole. Stick to a more neutral color scheme for your primary colors in a minimalist living room.

By using a neutral color palette, you can easily create visual emphasis with the lines and shapes, Thus attributing to a more modern and visually appealing living room. Just because a neutral color palette fits better in a minimalist living room doesn't mean you can't use bold colors.

You can use your bolder colors like red, orange, or bright green on things like couch pillows without throwing the entire living room out of balance. Just make sure you keep the 60/30/10 rule in mind. This means 60% of your living room color should be neutral, 30% for your secondary color, and 10% for your accent colors. Make sure your accent colors don't go over 10%, or it can threaten your entire neutral color palette.

Light colors often make a room look bigger than it is. If you have a living room on the smaller side, a softer tone of color will suit it better, but that doesn't mean you can't use dark colors at all. A darker color scheme helps enhance your focal point. For example, if you have arranged your living room around your couch, you can use a darker carpet/rug or coffee table to draw attention to the sofa and the space around it.

Step Three: Limit your wall decorations

Limit how many wall decorations you put up, like family photos or paintings. Too many wall decorations can make a room feel cramped and cluttered. When hanging things up, blank wall space can have the same impact as a living room with items hung on the walls.

Step Four: Incorporate floating shelves

Most people use bookshelves to store things like movies, CDs, and books in their living room. We suggest using floating shelves in a minimalist living room. These are more flexible, and you can put them anywhere, unlike a bookcase which is visually bulky and can take up so much visual space. With floating shelves, you also don't take up floor space, so your living room won't feel so cramped.

Step Five: Declutter your living room

The feeling of an open room is lost once clutter forms on your bookshelves, coffee tables, or even your end tables. Clutter can make any room smaller and much more cramped; that's why decluttering is an essential step in minimalist interior design.

Using furniture with multiple purposes will fit well in your minimalist home. For instance, you can use a coffee table with a hidden compartment to store things away; there are also couches nowadays with the same features.

Step Six: Just the right amount of lighting

By using proper lighting, you can create a dynamic yet minimalist living room with an emphasis on shapes, lines, neutral colors, and space. While neutral living does help, you risk your minimalist style looking bland and uninviting. As such, you will have to add more lighting throughout the living room to enhance the existing lighting.

For example, table and floor lamps. Floor lamps, strip lighting, and lighting in the form of wall sconces can help draw the eye to wall decorations or unique architectural details.

Step Seven: Implement mirrors

Mirrors are great for smaller living rooms. It not only reflects lighting but also makes the perception of the space feel bigger. Mirrors can function as modern decorative pieces in a minimalist lifestyle, and they can add more interest to your walls.

Step Eight: Add some plants and greenery

Because we focus on a modern style and neutral colors, it can feel a little cold and uninviting. Try adding some houseplants; they also have numerous benefits.

Adding neutral elements

Neutral elements are things like stones, wood, and plant life, which have a calming effect on the mind. They also give off a peaceful atmosphere. It's why the Japanese use neutral elements in their traditional interior design styles and are also very minimalistic.

Add color

A dash of green can be just what a neutral-colored living room needs to add some visual vibrancy and contrast without overwhelming the overall aesthetic.

Improve indoor air quality: Your interior design can affect indoor air quality. It can feel less relaxing, less comfortable, and messier. By adding indoor plants, you create a more pleasant environment to socialize or relax in, and you filter the air at the same time.

Step Nine: Have everything fit for a cohesive living room design

Living minimalistic is all about the less is more approach. Pick furniture and decor items that contribute to the overall aesthetic and ensure they complement each other and work well with the space.

Step Ten: Don't throw away your own personal style

There are multiple rules to follow when adopting a minimalist lifestyle. At first sight, it may look like minimalist design strips away all decorative flourishes, that it has no place in the design if it does not contribute to the overall aesthetic. As a result, you might think a minimalist design is a little much for your tastes.

However, there is no particular reason to sacrifice your own personal style to achieve a minimalist design. You can always add your own unique personal touches throughout your minimalist design. A minimalist design still needs a bit of contrast and accent decor to truly create balance. You can play with color patterns and living room decor while still maintaining a minimalist style.

Office

What do you require to deliver your best work? A clear mind, space to work, and positive energy to make you believe you can achieve what you set out to achieve. While creating an environment that caters to all these needs might seem impossible, there is one method that works.

Creating a minimalist office reduces stress and makes you enjoy your clean office environment. You can refer to the steps previously mentioned in part two, and you can look at these five tips to incorporate minimalism into your office.

Tip One: Go without paper

It's hard to get into a relaxed mindset when piles of paper surround you. You will find it challenging to get down to work if you can't even see your desk from underneath all of those documents. Going paperless can bring about many different benefits. Some of these benefits include better organization, cost-saving, and reducing your environmental footprint.

Tip Two: Purchase only what you require

You don't need 300 of each item. Buying in bulk might be the better choice to save you money, but it clutters your workspace if it just lays around not being used, not to mention it can make it look and feel crowded.

You rarely make it through the office supplies you've bought in bulk; here's what happens. You tend to waste your staples, pens, and so on just because you know you have extra. You will take more care of your office supplies if you know you don't have an endless amount lying around the office.

Tip Three: Use storage cleverly

Getting rid of all your items except the essentials is impossible. There will be things you need to have, but that means they don't have to take up all your space. Instead, you just need to use your storage cleverly. Use storage bins to store things that you cant keep in sight. This way, your office will always look neat and organized.

Tip Four: Limit the tech

In any office, you have certain technologies that get specific jobs done. Specifically speaking, when it comes to minimalist philosophy, it doesn't mean you can't incorporate technology. For starters, try and limit the bulky pieces of technology. Use a slim laptop instead of a large desktop computer.

Functionally, it's pretty much the same; aesthetically, it's much better. You might need one bulky piece of tech to fax and print, but it's better to have a machine that can do both simultaneously rather than two different ones.

Tip Five: limit your surrounding distractions

You should have a few pieces to brighten up your offices, such as a plant, maybe a sofa, or a giant clock, but that's about it. Try not to go overboard when choosing your accessories because it might serve as a distraction from what you're trying to achieve, which is a unified and minimalist workspace.

Gifts, sentimental objects, and heirlooms

When decluttering, you will come across items that bring you to a stop; they're neither beautiful nor valuable, yet you can't get yourself to throw them away. You didn't even choose to bring some of these items into your life. These are items like gifts, sentimental objects, and heirlooms.

Gifts

First, we have gifts. A gift is an object filled with a particular emotion or intention. Therefore set free the things you don't need and keep only the ones you love and cherish. If you receive a gift that is not up to your taste, put it in the donation box. It's the thought behind giving the gift that counts.

You don't have to make space for the present if you're not going to use it, simply take a photo with the present and send it to the person. Whether it's a sweater, scarf, or hand-knitted socks, you can donate the gift to your local charity or someone who truly needs it. This way, everyone will be happy.

Heirlooms

Next, we have heirlooms. When it comes to decluttering, antiques can be challenging to get rid of simply because the owner of the items is no longer with us. That fact alone scares us. But try to remember that the stuff isn't the person. It's just things they owned, just like the stuff you own.

Pass on such a family history; who knows, one of your other family members might want it? If the heirlooms are historically significant or valuable, donate them to your local history society or museum. If you plan on passing down heirlooms, remember that your children might not want them one day.

Unfortunately, heirlooms aren't the only sentimental objects we have to worry about; we often acquire our own sentimental things, milestones, and events all come to mind, even accessories. We often find it hard to declutter some of these things because it feels like parting with some of our memories.

We just need to understand that the events and experiences of our lives are not engraved on these objects. While things can be taken away or broken, the memories they represent will stay with or without them. With that in mind, let's consider a category that can get in our way while decluttering.

Sentimental items

A great example of sentimental items is items you accumulated for your wedding. Your wedding is likely to be the uppermost memorable event of your life. Therefore there is bound to be a lot of sentiment behind the items you accumulated. Choose a container and limit your wedding keepsakes to what will fit inside.

You don't have to store the entire bridal-themed clutter. Getting rid of a few items won't hurt either; rather than keeping them for years where they can get damaged, donate them to your local wedding venue; they might find a use for them again. If you plan on passing your wedding dress down, remember that your daughter might not want it by the time she gets married because something new is in fashion.

As you declutter, you will find items you are unsure of getting rid of and might want to keep. Put such items in a box or storage container and set a date to come back to them. If you've changed your mind by the time you get back to them, consider relocating them to a new home or donating them to someone in need.

Part Four: Your Daily Routine & the Environment

Minimalism and Your Mental Health

mental health

How does minimalism affect mental health?

Minimalism is often perceived as a holistic lifestyle; however, you can link both the benefits and the practices. The ideas behind getting rid of uneasy items are the same ideas that support changes in other areas of life. This makes it so that minimalists can grow in different ways by taking simple approaches.

For example, when it comes to getting rid of the physical, it's recommended people look for the things that are no longer valuable to them. This often includes getting rid of stuff you hardly ever notice. Such as odds and ends you forgot you had or things stuffed deep in the closet that you don't have any use for.

According to minimalism, there's no reason to hold onto things that don't serve a purpose in our everyday lives or provide us with some pleasure, whether it be a sentimental gift, nostalgic photo, or aesthetic piece of art. Many personal benefits have been linked to the practice of minimalism. The below mental health improvements have been brought to your attention in relation to the implementation of minimalistic practices.

Individual sovereignty

This mainly refers to feelings of individuality and independence. Those who implement the practice of minimalism into their lives are more likely to feel more comfortable and confident with themselves as individuals.

Competence

Minimalists can focus better on the task that requires their undivided attention because fewer distractions surround them. When it comes to interpersonal relationships or work assignments, individuals are more prone to attend to those crucial matters happening in their lives.

Awareness

Your capability goes hand in hand with understanding. Minimalists often notice things they haven't in the past when they pay attention to their surroundings. This makes them more observant and attentive, which has been linked to productivity in many areas of life, such as relationships and work.

Mental space

People who incorporate minimalist practices are, on average, more self-disciplined. They can dedicate their attention to one thing rather than multitasking. In this way, they can place all their efforts into the task at hand without getting distracted by unnecessary thoughts or objects.

Positive emotions

Overall, minimalists experience more fulfillment and happiness and less anxiety and stress. Because they can get more out of meaningful interactions and habits, they don't concern themselves with the minute details of everyday life.

How Can Minimalism Improve Work Productivity?

The same crucial principle can be used in other aspects of life. Discard habits that waste your time and discard things that don't bring you joy. When it comes to daily routines, minimalists often use the same ideas when pitching physical objects. Unless it brings you joy or is helpful, don't do it.

This mainly refers to habits we don't even realize, wasting significant amounts of our time, for instance, wasting hours on social media without receiving any actual value. It is essential to recognize that the point is not to be productive every second of the day; instead, spend your time on things that have some meaning.

For many minimalists, this includes following a similar schedule every day if their work and personal lives allow it, of course. We can focus more on each interaction, task, and its effects on us when we're not stressing about our ever-changing schedule. You will undoubtedly become more aware and see the vast potential and benefits that were previously discussed if you fully immerse yourself in each experience you have throughout your day.

Implementing minimalist practices can have many uses in a time when so many of us are working from home. Thinking about the work week, how often does each item in your workspace get addressed.? Does each object in your makeshift office serve some kind of purpose or elicit some type of positive emotion from you?

It's easy to ignore things when working in the same place every day. If you walk through your home, would you be able to remember the placement of each object? Would you even remember you had it to start with? If you're looking for ways to maximize your productivity, these can be helpful questions to ask yourself. The same goes for your everyday habits.

Here are five observations regarding the psychology behind minimalism and why we think it's taking over the world.

Effective stress reliever

Visual clutter has a way of trapping people in an endless cycle of anxiety. How many times have you looked at a pile of items and felt your resolve slowly creep away? I'll do it another day, you think. Little by little, it begins to undermine our mental health and personal wellness.

Some people tend to never break out of the cycle. Discarding things that no longer have any value to you will make you more productive and help you feel more at home. With fewer possessions, your items become easily accessible since you no longer have to search for them, and your home is easier to clean. You become more efficient, focus better, and are more selective about what you bring into your home.

We're becoming less materialistic

A study conducted in the (U.S.) The United States of America shows millennials opt for more fulfilling experiences rather than having materialistic possessions. This means that their social morals have changed. People realize that material things don't make them happy, and the joy of owning something new is often short-lived.

It's becoming more popular

With so much coverage, including videos, books, magazines, podcasts, and online courses, the practice of less is more has really been adopted worldwide. Minimalism has now been accepted as both a design aesthetic and a way of living. In this modern era, people often seek to eliminate unnecessary clutter from their lives.

At the same time, these same individuals are also motivated to achieve a clean, straightforward color scheme. This is especially true when attempting to keep up with the latest in minimalist design trends.

Paves the way for self actualization

It's easy to be swept up in today's modern consumerist culture. This is why it is vital to embrace minimalism, as it reminds you that there is more to life than our possessions. Minimalism encourages us to focus more on the things that contribute to our personal growth and less on the deficiencies in our basic needs—making sure that our needs are reasonable and not excessively satisfied.

We want to do what's right

Perhaps the critical reason for minimalism's rapid uptake in recent years is that excessive consumption harms the environment. From manufacturing to disposal, excessive consumption increases pollution and the demand for our Earth's limited natural resources.

Amongst those who follow an environmentally conscious way of living, many have also adopted the minimalist approach. This is primarily because minimalism is in alignment with their goals. Many of these individuals attempt to lead zero waste lives, and minimalism is an excellent way to start.

Create, Implement and Manage Your Schedule

During our quest to embrace minimalism, we first want to focus on the stuff that clutters our homes. We want to eliminate all the excess and reclaim our space so we have enough room to grow, live, learn, and play.

However, we also need enough time for such activities. Therefore, we must organize our schedules as well. This next section will look at six ways to minimize our to-dos and maximize our efficiency, thereby gaining a little more tranquility in our daily lives.

Say No!

Unfortunately, we can't please everyone, be everywhere simultaneously, or do everything. We only have a set amount of days in each week and hours in each day, and there comes a point where we have to learn to say no. Like each object takes up space in your home, so does each task in your schedule.

And your schedule might just be tight as it is; if you can say no, something has to give. Saying no to new tasks ensures that your current ones are not neglected, and the people who deserve your time still get it.

Eliminate all the excess

Sometimes we stop seeing our stuff when we have a lot of it cluttering up the place. We often find ourselves turning a blind eye to the current mess, telling ourselves we just don't have enough space. At the same time, we often fail to recognize the clutter in our schedules.

Our schedules are just like our shelves, drawers, and closets and can sometimes benefit from decluttering. Start fresh by looking at how you spend your day. Put commitment and every activity on paper so that you can see it for yourself.

List everything: going to work, shopping for groceries, watching television, getting your nails done, going for coffee, reading the newspaper, doing the laundry, cooking dinner, browsing websites, driving your daughter to ballet class, playing poker with your buddies, and anything else that occupies your hours.

Take a look at your daily schedule. Does it match your ideal one? Keeping this question in mind, browse through your current plan and begin removing any unessential activities. This means you must decide what tasks are vital and which can be trashed. Now I'm not suggesting you abandon the activities you enjoy but rather to take each one and gauge how important it is to you.

Prioritize

Sometimes we can get overwhelmed by our to-do list and everything on it. So we jump from one task to the next without reason, taking on each new chore as it pops into our heads. We are often busy trying to accomplish multiple objectives while worrying about what we aren't doing.

This often makes most of us panic, fearing that we won't accomplish anything. With that said, we have already started saying no to receiving or purchasing extra items; simultaneously, you have also eliminated any excess possessions. So what exactly is a minimalist supposed to do.

Herein lies the problem; it isn't generally about the size of the to-do list but rather that you don't know where to begin tackling the objectives. This is where the benefit of prioritizing comes in, as it allows you to create and make use of a well-rounded schedule. By following a schedule instead of aimlessly wandering around trying to do multiple tasks, you can rather accomplish one task at a time.

This means that when you learn to prioritize your responsibilities, you can take charge of your available time, and you are able to focus your attention on completing a task rather than stressing about it being incomplete. To achieve this level of prioritizing, the simplest way to go about it is to list your assignments by way of importance. Start by listing everything you need to accomplish, from most to least urgent.

Consolidate

Now that we have organized our spaces well, by making use of groups to sort our belongings, we can keep all of your similar objects together. You will come to find that you can store, purge and access your belongings far easier than before you began. In the same vein, you can also incorporate the same method to get your schedule organized.

You can do this by keeping all similar tasks grouped together. By doing so, you will be able to manage both your to-do list and the time required to achieve your tasks more efficiently. We can apply the same technique to all of our tasks: whether it's doing household chores, preparing food, completing work assignments, answering emails, scheduling appointments, or making phone calls.

By grouping similar jobs and tackling them simultaneously, we minimize the time needed for establishing, tidying, and implementing. Instead of doing a bit of ironing each night, do it all in one session. Or, instead of working on a project in bits and pieces, knock it out in as few sittings as possible. Instead of returning phone calls throughout the day, schedule a time to do them all at once.

Delegate

Most of us have a full plate between family, household responsibilities, and work. Even after getting rid of most of the clutter on our to-do list, we sometimes feel like we still don't have enough hours in our day. In this case, we must realize that we can't do it ourselves and learn to delegate tasks to others.

This technique is particularly effective in the office. If you're lucky enough to have staff, consider delegating more of your responsibilities to them. It lifts your burdens and helps your employees develop the skills to move to the next level. Delegation can be especially beneficial if you're running your own business.

As an entrepreneur, you're likely "doing it all." In addition to your day-to-day responsibilities, you may be completing your tax returns, creating your own website, designing your own advertising, writing your own press releases, handling client inquiries, and trimming the hedges outside your store or office.

Consider sharing some of these responsibilities with outside contractors or employees; it can free up significant time to grow and develop your business. If you're concerned about the cost, realize that your time is more valuable than what you pay someone to mow your lawn or do your taxes.

Of course, the main problem when delegating tasks is perfectionism. We feel that nobody else can do the job as well as we can; we insist on doing everything ourselves. In the next section, we'll discuss the solution: recognizing that not everything has to be done perfectly.

Embrace 'just enough.'

Have you ever spent a significant portion of your time preparing an excellent presentation, finding the perfect gift, writing the perfect email, or cooking the perfect dinner? The quest for perfection can throw our to-do lists out of balance; what we should have been able to complete in a short time takes us two, three, or four times as long!

In 99 percent of the things we do, perfection is redundant. It's unnecessary, unexpected, and likely won't be appreciated or noticed. So here we are, devoting extra effort and time to making everything just so—and nobody cares. It's a beautiful realization; when we stop striving for perfection, we get our stuff done faster and more efficiently.

We end up zooming through our to-do lists more quickly than you expected. Accept "good enough" for the work you delegate and don't redo an employee's report because you think you can make it better. By recognizing that perfection isn't always necessary, you'll increase productivity and free up your mind and schedule for things that truly matter.

Environmental Minimalism and Its Benefits

How to benefit the environment though minimalism

There's a change that comes upon us when we become minimalists. All the hard work you put in along the way has finally come true. Whenever we decide against a frivolous purchase, borrow from a friend or make do with something we already have instead of buying, it's like giving a little gift to the planet.

The water will be a little clearer, the air a little cleaner, the landfills a little emptier, and the forests a little fuller. We may have embraced minimalism to save time, money, or space in our homes. Still, our actions have far more significant benefits: they protect the Earth from environmental harm and save people from suffering unsafe and unfair working conditions.

Our consumption has both an ecological and human toll. Before buying, we must consider a product's life cycle to ensure its purchase won't do more harm than good. With that in mind, let's discuss some further minimalist habits we can use to lighten our footprint on the planet and conserve its natural resources for future generations.

Become a 'minsumer'

Corporations, politicians, and advertisers like to define us as "consumers." By encouraging us to buy as much as possible, they line their pockets, grow their profits, and get reelected. Where does that leave us? Putting in overtime to purchase things that'll be out of style or obsolete in months.

Drinking dirty water and breathing polluted air so retailers can fill their shelves with more widgets and corporate executives can take home bigger bonuses. But there's some fantastic news: minimalist living sets us free! It unbinds us from the " spend and work " cycle, enabling us to create an existence that has little to do with must-have items, finance charges, or big box stores.

We can become "minsumers" instead of laboring away as consumers, minimizing the impact of our consumption on the environment, lessening the effect of our consumption on other people's lives, and minimizing our consumption to what meets our needs.

Whenever we ignore television commercials, borrow books from the library, breeze by impulse items without a glance, resist purchasing the latest electronic gadget, or mend our clothes instead of replacing them, we're committing our own little acts of "consumer disobedience." By simply not buying, we accomplish a world of good: we avoid supporting exploitative labor practices and reclaim our planet's resources, delivering them from the hands of corporations into those of our children and the future generations.

Reduce

We're all familiar with the words" Reuse, Reduce, Recycle." Recycling a media darling and the superstar. It prominently features in community programs and environmental campaigns. It's usually the focal point of our efforts when deciding to go green. However, reducing is the unsung hero of this group because the less we buy in the first place, the less we have to recycle!

Consolidating sidesteps the entire energy -and resource- and labor-intensive process and is, therefore, the cornerstone of our consumer philosophy. There are three critical aspects in every product that we buy's life cycle. These aspects include production, distribution, and disposal. In the production phase, natural energy and resources are used to make the item.

In some cases, harmful chemicals are released into the water and air as a byproduct of the manufacturing process. In the distribution phase, energy, typically in the form of oil for ships, trucks, and airplanes, is used to transport the item from the factory to the store. These days that often means a trip halfway around the world! In the disposal phase, the item leaches toxins into the environment as it degrades and has the potential to clog our landfills.

By recycling, we're trying to do some "damage control" by avoiding its disposal problems and using its material to make new goods. On the other hand, reducing eliminates the entire troublesome process. Each item we don't buy is one less thing to be produced, distributed, and disposed of.

Reuse

Reuse is at the center of our minsumer efforts. The longer we can keep a particular item in service, the better, especially if it prevents us from buying something new. Since resources have already been devoted to its production and distribution, we are responsible for getting the most use possible from it.

While recycling requires extra energy to make something new, reusing requires none. In its original form, we adapt the product to meet different needs. We have plenty of opportunities to reuse things regularly: like the packaging materials, we receive boxes, bubble wrap, packing peanuts, wrapping paper, ribbons, and bows on our gifts.

Of course, as minimalists, we don't want to clutter our drawers and cabinets with stuff we might never use. Therefore, if you don't require something, give it to someone who does. Reuse doesn't automatically mean you have to reuse it; the planet will be just as well off if somebody else does.

Recycle

Our ultimate goal as minsumers is to live lightly on the Earth, putting as little into landfills as possible using fewer resources. Our main objective is to reduce our consumption to the bare minimum, and our second is to reuse whatever we can. However, we'll still end up with items that are no longer useful; and in those cases, we should make every effort possible to recycle them.

In recent years recycling has become much more straightforward. This has allowed various communities to create their own curbside collection initiatives for metal, glass, select plastic, and paper. Other communities have adopted a similar approach by forming and maintaining a drop-off location or locations for recyclable waste resources available to you; why not make use of them.

Remember, when we buy an item, we take responsibility for its entire life cycle, including its proper disposal. Although recycling usually occurs at the end of a product's life cycle, keep it in mind from the beginning. When you're shopping, favor products that you can recycle over those that can't.

Avoid acquiring toxic and hazardous materials like oils, cleaners, pesticides, and paints, because improper disposal of such dangerous items is harmful to the environment and a threat to our health; you'll need to drop them off at particular collection sites to get rid of them. Take the easy way out, and seek non-toxic, safer products to meet your household demands.

Consider reusing someone else's stuff for your needs

Say you've been invited to a wedding and don't have an appropriate outfit. Before you hit the department stores, try to find something pre-owned: check out the charity shops and thrift stores in your area, and search online auctions and classifieds. Failing that, raid the closets of relatives and friends or use a rental service.

Do the same for furniture, tools, electronics, and almost anything you can think of; regard the secondhand market as your default source, and only buy retail as a last resort. You'll avoid putting additional pressure on our overtaxed environment and prevent something valuable from ending up in the trash.

6 Benefits of Minimalism & The Environment Affect

Preserving natural resources

You will consume less naturally and only buy what you need as you become more mindful about your spending habits. Earth's non-renewable resources are finite and valuable. The continuous usage of gas, plastic, and similar non-recyclable products might lead to a deficiency in these resources; however, if you reuse all your old wrapping papers or giant plastic containers, you can preserve Earth's natural resources.

Reducing waste

Living a Minimalist lifestyle involves spending less on food, clothes, etc. As you buy less, you will waste less. Although these products appear to be too insignificant to cause real damage, they might get accumulated over time and fill landfills.

Living in smaller homes

Living in a smaller house helps prevent air pollution and reduce CO_2 emissions because we consume less energy on things such as lighting, heating, etc. Minimalism is eco-friendlier, especially with more people adapting to the lifestyle. The core meaning behind minimalism teaches us to choose what is of most value while removing anything that takes up space or is deemed clutter.

Letting go of perfection

Every individual wants the choice of having perfect objects. However, as an eco-friendly minimalist, remember that perfection comes at a heavy financial or environmental price. Buy hand-crafted and natural products instead of overspending.

Prevent noise pollution

You will save more money on parking, oil change maintenance, and gas for your car when you walk more often instead of driving everywhere. Besides, it also helps prevent the release of harmful smoke into the environment and noise pollution.

Making eco-friendly decisions

By opting to take on and embrace minimalist living, you can attain the ability to achieve a multitude of decisions in an eco-friendly manner. Such choices include carpooling to work, canceling catalog subscriptions, and reducing shower times.

How You Can Use Minimalism to Make a Difference

Several environmental benefits to minimalism can be achieved without negatively impacting your life. For example, considering the lifespan, considering the materials, and buying local are easy ways to ensure that your purchases don't contribute as much to climate change.

Consider the lifespan

As minsumers, we aim to purchase as little as possible; therefore, we want the things we buy to last a long time. We must consider the lifespan of an item in our decision to acquire it. Why waste all those precious resources on a product we have had for a few months? For this reason, choose items that are durable and well-made. When you're shopping, comparing prices is easy, but it can be difficult to determine quality.

How do you know if that chair will collapse next month or if that watch will stop ticking next week? You have to look for clues: like where the product was made, the materials it's constructed of, and the manufacturer's reputation. Although price isn't always a gauge of quality, low cost isn't typically associated with longevity. While replacing the item may not break the bank, we must consider the environmental costs.

Refrain from purchasing trendy items, like the décor that'll look outdated next season, the handbag that's "hot" one moment and "not" a few minutes later, or those electronic gadgets that'll be obsolete in a few months. Instead, classic items that'll stay in style forever or choose pieces you genuinely love; then, you'll be able to measure their lifespan in decades rather than days.

Unfortunately, "single-use" stuff has become increasingly popular in our society: from razors to plates, diapers to napkins, cleaning cloths to cameras. Many such items are used daily and can generate tremendous waste. You can slash your carbon footprint dramatically by favoring reusable versions: like canvas shopping bags, handkerchiefs, proper tableware and utensils, rechargeable batteries, cloth napkins, diapers, and towels. As usual, let the lifespan be your guide; look for a longer-lasting alternative if it's ridiculously short.

Consider the materials

When evaluating your purchase, consider the materials from which it was made. By choosing items produced with renewable or sustainable resources, you can minimize the impact of your consumption. As a general rule, favor products made from natural materials over manufactured ones. Synthetic substances like plastics are typically made from petroleum, a non-renewable resource.

The manufacturing process is energy-intensive; it exposes workers to hazardous fumes and chemicals that can emit harmful toxins. Furthermore, some plastics contain additives that can leach into water and food and pose a health risk. Disposal presents an additional problem. Plastics degrade slowly and can persist in landfills for hundreds or even thousands of years; on the other hand, burning them can create toxic air pollution.

Natural materials don't require the same energy inputs and are significantly easier to dispose of and recycle. But buying something made of wood doesn't mean we're in the clear. We must still be vigilant concerning its harvesting and origin. Large swaths of land have been deforested to produce furniture, paper, lumber flooring, and other products. Unsustainable harvesting and illegal logging have destroyed ecosystems, altered local climates, and displaced indigenous tribes.

To avoid contributing to such tragedies, look for wood that has been certified as coming from sustainable sources, and favor rapidly renewable types like bamboo over endangered species like teak and mahogany. Reduce your environmental impact by purchasing products made from recycled content. You'll find paper, clothing, handbags, shoes, flooring, décor, furniture, glassware, jewelry, and plenty of other items enjoying a second life as something new.

Buying recycled goods preserves natural resources, saves energy, and prevents the original items from ending in landfills. Show your minsumer spirit, and take pride in whether your dining table is from reclaimed wood or your tote bag was made from soda bottles. Finally, consider the packaging. The ideal, of course, is none, especially considering the brevity of its lifespan.

However, many of the items we buy will come with some outer casing. Favor those products that can easily be recycled or with the least amount of packaging. And by all means, make it a habit to use cloth bags instead, don't bring home your purchases in a plastic bag. This action alone can save an incredible amount of waste and energy!

Buy local

We've talked a lot about production and disposal and how we can minimize our footprints concerning them. However, we must also consider distribution and how the transport of goods from where they're made to where we buy them adds to their environmental toll. Much of the stuff in our households originated halfway around the globe. The problem is the additional energy, in the form of fuel, must be expended to transport it.

Oil is a non-renewable energy source that gets scarcer each day. Yet, we fill up planes, ships, and trucks with it to move consumer goods from one corner of the world to another instead of conserving them. Unfortunately, that means fewer resources in our future and more pollution in our atmosphere. Is it worth the environmental consequences of sending a mini skirt or a mango on a two-thousand-mile journey? Not to us minsumers.

We prefer to buy our goods locally, clean our air, and save energy. Instead, we'd purchase chairs from a local craftsperson rather than a furniture superstore; décor from the community art fair instead of a global retailer; and our clothes from a clothes shop in our own country. When we buy locally, we not only save the environment; we also strengthen our communities. Instead of sending our hard-earned money to foreign countries, we put them right back into our communities.

Here they can provide the services, build infrastructure, and fund the needed programs required by the community. We save our farmland from developers, preserving agricultural traditions and open space. Best of all, we build long-lasting, personal relationships with the people who supply our stuff. It's lovely to know that our consumption is helping a local merchant's child attend college or a farmer maintain his livelihood, rather than paying the bonus of some distant corporate executive.

Conclusion

Everyone has their reasons for choosing a minimalist lifestyle. Perhaps you picked up this book because your rooms are cluttered, your drawers are stuffed, and your closets are bursting at the seams. Maybe you realized that shopping at the mall, and acquiring new things, isn't making you happy.

Or maybe you're concerned about the effects of your current consumption on the environment and worried that your children and grandchildren wouldn't have the clean water and air that should be their birthright. I hope that the advice on these pages has inspired you to declutter your home, simplify your life, and live a little more lightly on the Earth.

I hope that the advice on these pages has inspired you to declutter your home, simplify your life, and live a little more lightly on the Earth. It's a message you won't hear in our "more is better" society; you'll almost always hear the opposite. Everywhere we turn, we're encouraged to consume often by magazines, commercials, radio, billboards, and ads on buses, buildings, bathroom stalls, benches, and even in our schools. With minimalist living comes freedom from debt and clutter. Each extraneous thing you remove from your life, whether an unnecessary purchase, unfulfilling, or unused item, feels like a weight lifted from your shoulders.

You'll have fewer errands to run and less to pay for, shop for, maintain, clean, and insure. You'll feel fancy-free and footloose: able to pursue opportunities without fussing over all your stuff and move on a dime. Moreover, when you're not chasing status symbols or keeping up with other people, you gain energy and time for more fulfilling pursuits: like participating in your community and playing with your kids or family.

We fill our lives with unessential items, activities (whether personal or work-related), and clutter. When we let our lives become too full, we often forget to make the necessary room for more experiences and opportunities to deepen our relationships and broaden our opportunistic chances to grow ourselves further.

By embracing and adopting a minimalist lifestyle, you can help fix this. When you start by eliminating all the unnecessary items from your home, office, and schedule, you allow yourself to free up your mind and more time. This allows you to enjoy what matters most in your life; love, hope, exorbitant amounts of joy, and the ability to truly live.

Made in the USA
Las Vegas, NV
02 November 2023

80122547R00049